3 -50

I wish to thank my wife for her help a   whilst
compiling this book. I also wish to th   valued
assistance and support.
I must also thank all the Brigades, Brigade personnel, and County Council's who
have assisted me, by supplying me with the information that I requested of them.

Foreword.

To the new collector of Cap Badges there are many unknowns, the following is an outline of the classes of British Fires Services Cap Badges:-

Pre 1974 Cap Badges.

These date from 1947 when the National Fire Service was de-nationalised and the brigades handed back to local councils. The Local Government Act of 1972 abolished from 1st April 1974 the local councils many small brigades were therefore amalgamated together to form one large brigade, with in most cases a new name and cap badge, hence many badges disappeared forever.

The pre badges are divided into two separate groups, (1) County Borough Brigades, (2) County Brigades. There were 86 County Borough Brigades and 78 County Fire Brigades, many of the badges of these brigades had variations, ie. Coat of Arms, Shield, in chrome and/or gilt and so on. Previously unknown variations of these badges are still turning up today, which makes the collecting of these badges still more exciting for the collector.

Post 1974 Cap Badges.

These are the badges of the newly formed brigades following the Local Government Reorganisation in 1974, to the present day. Of these there are 57 brigades, again with many variations. In the last few years, many brigades are adopting the now popular title of 'Fire and Rescue Service', in recognition of the wider role now being played by the service in rescue operations.

Michael Akers.
Author.

The origins of the badge can be traced back many hundreds of years to the days of the Lords and Barons. The badge was originally a distinctive mark worn by servants, retainers and followers who were below the rank of gentlemen and therefore had no right to bear arms themselves. The badge was a means of identifying them with their master, and was very often derived from his Coat of Arms or the Crest above it.

From this early beginning the badge has developed into a symbol, to some even a status, a belonging.

The design of the eight pointed star goes back into history, the eight pointed star is the cross of St. John, it originated in the Maltese Cross, the Emblem of the Knights of Malta, and was used by the Knights of St. John of Jerusalem at the time of The Crusades. The points or 'tenets' were said to represent the knightly virtues of tact, perseverence, gallantry, loyalty, dexterity, explicitness, observation and sympathy. All Fire Service Badges are mounted onto various eight pointed star designs.

The different parts and points of an heraldic shield are distinguished and entitled as follow:

A Dexter side   H Dexter base
B Sinister side J Siniser base
C Chief   K Middle base
D Base   L Honour point
E Dexter chief   M Fess point
F Sinister chief N Nombril or Navel
G Middle chief   point

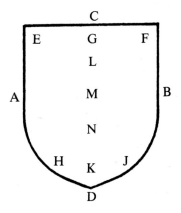

The above is reproduced from the publication 'Boutell's Heraldry' by J.P. Brook-Little, with the kind permission of Frederick Warne (Publishers) limited.

Author's Note

Collectors will note that there is a difference between the 'Official' brigade title and the badge title in some brigades. This is because some brigades use the word 'County' in their official title but delete it from the badge title.
MA.

Volumn one...Cap badges from 1974 to present day.
Volumn two...Cap badges from 1947 to 1974. (To follow)

Artistic work by firefighter Chris Reynolds.

The facts in this book are as supplied to the author and so published in good faith.

Published by: M.A. Akers, 14 Gladstone Avenue, Feltham, Middlesex, TW14 9LL, England.

Standard Book Number.

INDEX

FB.   Fire Brigade.
F & RS.   Fire & Rescue Service.
FS.   Fire Service.

1. *Brigade:* **COUNTY OF AVON FIRE BRIGADE.**

2. **Date formed:** 1st April 1974.

3. *Brigades amalgamated:* City of Bath, City and County of Bristol, Bath fire & ambulance service, parts of Somerset and Gloucestershire fire brigades.

4. *Badge design:* Home Office Star. red ring, chrome and enamel sea stag in white. The sea stag is the county badge and not the full County Arms. The Sea Stag i.e. stags with fishtails is a support to the coat of arms. They represent the fusion of two characteristic features of Avon - sea and forest. The historic importance of the Avon ports is linked with that of the royal forests which covered a large part of the County. Each stag is a 'stag royal', i.e. with six tines on each antler, and has about the neck an ancient crown of fleurs-de-lis to emphasise the royal association. On the shoulder of the sea stag is a roundel of six white and blue waves, again representing the rivers and springs of the County.

5. *Badge worn by:* Same badge worn by all ranks.

6. *Badge fixing:* Loops and pin.

7. *Badge manufacturer:* Smith and Wright Ltd.

8. *Badge design shown on uniform buttons:* Yes

   Badge design shown on appliances: No. Full County Crest.

9. *Other particulars:* 1st Issue. Sea stag nearly all chrome.

   2nd Issue. Slightly larger red ring, sea stag has enameled bottom half.

1. *Brigade:* **BEDFORDSHIRE FIRE SERVICE**

2. **Date formed:** 1947

3. *Brigades amalgamated:* 1974 Luton Fire Brigade.

4. *Badge design:* Home Office Star, red ring, gilt and enamel shield. The Coat of Arms is derived from the Beauchamps, the leading family in the County after the Norman Conquest, and who were constables of Bedford Castle. The Beauchamp of 1215 was one of the promoters of Magna Carta. The wavy lines on the shield and the swan's neck rearing from a wreath of oak denotes the River Ouse. The vertical black column on the shield contains three gold escallops which commemorates the service of the House of Russell to the state, the County and the County Council, and is taken from the arms of that family. The lion supporting the shield is also taken from a similar supporter to the Russell Coat of Arms.
The supporter on the other side of the shield is a bull, denoting the importance of agriculture in the Country.
The motto, constant Be, is from John Bunyan's hymn "Who would true valor see, let him come hither, One here will constant be, come wind, come weather."

5. *Badge worn by:* Same badge worn by all ranks.

6. *Badge fixing:* Loop and pin.

7. *Badge manufacturer:* London Badge Ltd.

8. *Badge design shown on uniform buttons:* Yes

   Badge design shown on appliances: Yes

9. *Other particulars:* There have been three issues since 1947.

   1st Issue. . .1947/50 Black and Gold.

   2nd Issue. . .   Chrome, red ring.

   3rd Issue. . .   Enamel sh.

1. *Brigade:* **ROYAL BERKSHIRE FIRE AND RESCUE SERVICE.**

2. **Date formed:** 1974

3. *Brigades amalgamated:* Berks and Reading Fire Brigade, part of Buckinghamshire.

4. *Badge design:* Home Office Star, red ring, chrome enamel Coat of Arms in blue. The arms display two royal lions, appropriate because Berkshire is the royal county. These royal lions are also to be found in the former Eton urban district and have association with Reading Abbey, which was founded by Henry 1. The embattled border to the shield is intended to represent the castles of Berkshire, of which Windsor is the best known survivor. The lion support, on left of shield, is another royal symbol, and Henry VI's association with the founding of Eton college is acknowledged by the Tudor Rose (which joined the rose of Lancashire and the white rose of York) on the Lion's collar.
The horse support, on the right of the shield, represents the county's considerable connection with horse racing. There is a six pointed star on the collar of this supporter, refering to the six borough and districts in the county, and also to the close association of Slough with the celebrated astronomer Sir William Herschel.
The crest is based upon the badge of the old Militai, and there is a tradition that a banner with this symbol, or one similar, was carried by the men of Berkshire at the battle of Agincourt. The stag under the oak tree is assumed to represent the stags and the oaks of Windsor Forest.

5. *Badge worn by:* Same badge worn by all ranks.

6. *Badge fixing:* Loop and pin.

7. *Badge manufacturer:* Gaunt and Sons.

8. *Badge design shown on uniform buttons:* Yes old design

   Badge design shown on appliances: Yes old design

9. *Other particulars:* On the 1st July 1985 the brigade changed its title from 'Royal Berkshire fire brigade' to its present name. A new badge is to be issued.

1. *Brigade:* **BUCKINGHAMSHIRE FIRE BRIGADE**

2. **Date formed:** Same Brigade since 1948.

3. *Brigades amalgamated:* None

4. *Badge design:* Home Office Star., chrome metal painted badge. White ring, on a red background stands a swan in white, with a crown around its neck. The swan is taken from the Coat of Arms of the Duke of Buckingham. 1st Issue. Cream instead of white, badge covered in plastic. 2nd Issue. Gilt badge (appx. 250 issued), issued in 1983. 3rd Issue. Chrome. Issued in 1974.

5. *Badge worn by:* Same badge worn by all ranks.

6. *Badge fixing:* Loop and pin.

7. *Badge manufacturer:* Gaunt & Sons Ltd.

8. *Badge design shown on uniform buttons:* Yes

   Badge design shown on appliances: Yes

9. *Other particulars:* The change from plastic front to metal front was because the plastic cover tended to become detached from the badge.

1. *Brigade:* **CAMBRIDGESHIRE FIRE AND RESCUE SERVICE**

2. **Date formed:** 1974

3. *Brigades amalgamated:* Cambridge and Isle of Ely, and Huntingdon and Peterborough fire brigades.

4. *Badge design:* Home Office Star, gilt and enamel, with a scroll. The badge of the Cambridgeshire Fire and Rescue Service was unique in that it was the only fire service badge in the country which incorporates rescue in its title. The crown represents the diocese of Ely, Peterborough and Northampton. On the badge itself the wavy lines denote the rivers Ouse and Nene and the straight line the Fens, both a source of prosperity and development for the county.

5. *Badge worn by:* All ranks wear the same badge.

6. *Badge fixing:* Single arm.

7. *Badge manufacturer:* London Badge Co Ltd.

8. *Badge design shown on uniform buttons:* No

   Badge design shown on appliances: Yes

9. *Other particulars:*

1. *Brigade:* **CHESHIRE FIRE BRIGADE**

2. **Date formed:** 1974

3. *Brigades amalgamated:* Cheshire County fire brigade, Chester City fire service, Warrington County Borough fire brigade, part Lancashire fire brigade.

4. *Badge design:* Home Office Star, red ring, gilt enamel shield. Blue shield containing three bales of wheat and a sword, all in gilt. The exact reason for the shield design is unknown but the design has been traced back as early as 1580 on a print of a plan of the City of Chester. This design has now earned official recognition, in the arms of the County.

5. *Badge worn by:* Same badge worn by all ranks.

6. *Badge fixing:* Loop and pin.

7. *Badge manufacturer:*

8. *Badge design shown on uniform buttons:* No

   Badge design shown on appliances: No. Full County Arms.

9. *Other particulars:*

1. *Brigade:* **CLEVELAND COUNTY FIRE BRIGADE**

2. **Date formed:** 1974

3. *Brigades amalgamated:* Teesside & Hartlepool C.B. FB's. Part N. Riding C.B.F.B. Middlesborough FB.

4. *Badge design:* Home office star. Gilt and enamel shield over a scroll. Chief of Shield...left cogwheel represents the engineering industry, centre...an ancient ship alludes to the area's shipping connection. Right...a hexagon (the benzene symbol) the petrol - chemical industry. Main shield shows a lion taken from the arms of the Bruce family, closely associated with the Cleveland area, with a collar & crown found in the ensigns of the now extinct Dukes of Cleveland. The Lion is shown breathing flames "To symbolise the energy industry generally".

5. *Badge worn by:* Same badge worn by all ranks.

6. *Badge fixing:* Loop and pin.

7. *Badge manufacturer:*

8. *Badge design shown on uniform buttons:* Yes. Part only 'Lion'

   Badge design shown on appliances: Yes. Coat of Arms.

9. *Other particulars:*

1. *Brigade:* **CORNWALL COUNTY FIRE BRIGADE**

2. **Date formed:** 1974 (Same design since 1947)

3. ***Brigades amalgamated:*** None

4. ***Badge design:*** Home Office Star, chrome enamel shield, blue scroll. In the centre of the shield on a blue background, 15 silver balls set in five rows. The balls (bezants) are a direct link with the days when Cornwall was an independent Earldom, Cadoc, Earl of Cornwall at the time of the Norman invasion had for his arms "a black shield garnished with golden bosses or roundels". On the outer edge on a chrome background seven blue patches which represent the sea, and differences the arms from those of the Duchy. On the top edge a wreath with a Cornish raven resting its right claw upon a Coronet.

5. ***Badge worn by:*** Same badge worn by all ranks.

6. ***Badge fixing:*** Loop and pin.

7. ***Badge manufacturer:*** Gaunt and Son

8. ***Badge design shown on uniform buttons:*** Yes

   Badge design shown on appliances: Yes

9. ***Other particulars:*** 1st Issue (1948) Chrome enamel scroll. 2nd Issue Red enamel scroll. 3rd Issue (1974) Black enamel scroll.

1. *Brigade:* **CUMBRIA COUNTY FIRE SERVICE**

2. **Date formed:** 1974

3. ***Brigades amalgamated:*** Cumberland and Westmorland fire brigades, County Borough brigades of Carlisle and Barrow-in-Furness. Part of Lancashire and West Riding fire brigades.

4. ***Badge design:*** Home Office Star, large chrome enamel shield and scroll. The shield consists of a shield within a shield, the inner shield contains four vertical lines of blue, yellow, and green with two horizontal lines of chrome, blue and green.
   The outer shield contains three Parnassus flowers and three roses, all in chrome on a green background. On top of the shield is a wall in the shape of a crown.

5. ***Badge worn by:*** Same badge worn by all ranks.

6. ***Badge fixing:*** Loop and pin.

7. ***Badge manufacturer:*** Firmin and son

8. ***Badge design shown on uniform buttons:*** No. Full County Crest.

Badge design shown on appliances: No. Full Country Crest.

9. ***Other particulars:*** 1st Issue...Small shield.
   2nd Issue...Large shield. (both same design).

1. *Brigade:* **DERBYSHIRE FIRE SERVICE**

2. **Date formed:** 1974

3. *Brigades amalgamated:* Derby Borough & Derby County fire brigade.

4. *Badge design:* Home Office Star, gilt and enamel coat of arms, scroll. On the shield, a Tudor rose with three stags' heads above. The rose was taken from the centuries old county badge, and the stags' heads from the Cavendish arms by permission of the Duke of Devonshire.
The supporters in gilt, a stag and a ram, have special significance for Derbyshire. Deer are very closely associated with the county, founded by the Danish invaders of the ninth century, who named their first fort, Derby, for the wild deer were so abundant in the area. Sheep were introduced in the New Stone Age. They were a foundation of local farming, and later provided the raw material of the early cloth and leather industry on which many of the county's towns are based. The ram was the county's regimental mascot.
A top the shield, the dragon of the crest, with metal collar and pick, symbolizes the county's foundation by the Danes, men of the dragon ships, and county's mining and engineering enterprise. Dragons traditionally amass underground and guard great mineral wealth. The crest all in gilt.

5. *Badge worn by:* Same badge worn by all ranks.

6. *Badge fixing:* Loop and pin.

7. *Badge manufacturer:* Gaunt and son

8. *Badge design shown on uniform buttons:* Yes

Badge design shown on appliances: Yes

9. *Other particulars:* The present design was issued in 1983, before this the old Derbyshire badge from 1947 was retained from 1974/83. This was a red ring, chrome shield.

1. *Brigade:* **DEVON FIRE BRIGADE**

2. **Date formed:** 1973

3. *Brigades amalgamated:* Plymouth City and Exeter City fire brigades with Devon County fire service.

4. *Badge design:* Home Office Star, red ring, chrome enamel Coat of Arms. The field and lion crowned is a device alleged to have been granted to Devon in the 13th Century by Richard, Earl of Cornwall, King of the Romans and brother of Henry III, the charge occurs on a title found in Crediton church. The red lion is appropriate to the red soil of the County. The shield commemorates the sea, indentified by the blue colour, and the great part that is has played in the development of Devon and its seafarers, the most famous which was Sir Francis Drake. His little ship 'The Golden Hind' is featured on the shield. Sir Francis Drakes motto 'Auxilio Divino' - (By Divine Help) has been adopted, it was given to Sir Francis by Queen Elizabeth I when he undertook his great sea voyage. Also, the shield portrays the Lion of England in rampant position.
The shield is supported in the upright position on the symbolic green fields of Devon, by the red Devon Bull to signify the great agricultural involvement within the Country. Also the Wessex Wyvern, a mythical land and sea creature.
The Wyvern was used by the Kings of Wessex on their coats of arms when the Kingdom of Wessex was a predominant part of England.
The crest is surmounted by the head of a Dartmoor pony with a sprig of heather in its mouth. Symbolic of the County's main physical characteristic -the vast expanse of the two National Parks - Dartmoor and Exmoor. The head of the pony rests on the Naval Crown and this crown is included to commemorate the historical association of Devon with the 'Royal Navy'.

5. *Badge worn by:* Senior Officer...standard badge with oak wreath backing. Other ranks...standard metal badge.

6. *Badge fixing:* Loop and pin.

7. *Badge manufacturer:* Dowler Ltd

8. *Badge design shown on uniform buttons:* Yes

   Badge design shown on appliances: Yes

9. *Other particulars:*

1. *Brigade:* **DORSET FIRE BRIGADE.**

2. **Date formed:** 1974.

3. *Brigades amalgamated:* Bournemouth FB. and part Hampshire Fire Brigades.

4. *Badge design:* Home Office Star, red ring, Chrome shield. On the shield granted to the Dorset County Council in 1950, the three Lions on the shield of the arms are taken from the design of the seal formely used by the Council from its incorporation in 1888. In the base a Fleur-de-lys.

5. *Badge worn by:* Same badge worn by all ranks.

6. *Badge fixing:* Loops and pin.

7. *Badge manufacturer:* Various.

8. *Badge design shown on uniform buttons:* Yes

   Badge design shown on appliances: Yes.

9. *Other particulars:*

1. *Brigade:* **DURHAM COUNTY FIRE BRIGADE.**

2. **Date formed:** 1st April 1974.

3. *Brigades amalgamated:* Darlington Fire Brigade.

4. *Badge design:* Home Office Star, gilt and enamel shield and scroll.The arms are based on those granted to the former Durham County Council with the addition of a white rose. The Council had used the Arms of the Bishopric of Durham because the Council could be said to have succeeded, in some measure, to the palatinate jurisdiction formerly enjoyed by the palatine Bishops of Durham. In order to stress this succession the lions were depicted in the Grant of Arms as grasping swords and wearing on their heads coronets used by the Bishops in conjunction with the mitre. The cross is charged with 4 black diamonds which represent the coal and the industries dependent upon it. The white rose represents the former parts of the North Riding of Yorkshire. The Mural Crown in the manner normally reserved for County Councils.

5. *Badge worn by:* Same badge worn by all ranks.

6. *Badge fixing:* Loops and pin.

7. *Badge manufacturer:* London badge Co Ltd.

8. *Badge design shown on uniform buttons:* No as 1969 cap badge.

   Badge design shown on appliances: Yes.

9. *Other particulars:*

1. *Brigade:* **ESSEX COUNTY FIRE AND RESCUE SERVICE**

2. **Date formed:** 1974

3. *Brigades amalgamated:* Southend-on-sea County Borough fire brigade.

4. *Badge design:* Home Office Star, gilt enamel shield and scroll.
   A red shield on which three curved short sword-knives, with gilt handles (hilts) terminating in knobs (pomels) are placed one above the other with the points pointing to the right of the observer. A semi-circular notch is hollowed out of the back of each blade. Such weapons are known in heraldry as SEAXES, and their present form has been evoloped from the ancient Saxon short sword or sword knife. It is not at all clear why Essex adopted the three seaxes, but these arms have been traced back as far as the 17th Century.

5. *Badge worn by:* Same badge worn by all ranks.

6. *Badge fixing:* Loop and pin.

7. *Badge manufacturer:* London badge co Ltd.

8. *Badge design shown on uniform buttons:* Yes

   Badge design shown on appliances: Yes

9. *Other particulars:* From the 14th May 1985 the brigade change its name from 'Essex County Fire Brigade' to its present name. A new badge design is to follow. The Essex brigade has had the same design since 1947, issued in gilt and chrome.

1. *Brigade:* **GLOUCESTERSHIRE FIRE AND RESCUE SERVICE**

2. **Date formed:** 1974.

3. *Brigades amalgamated:* Gloucester City fire service.

4. *Badge design:* Home Office Star. gilt and enamel coat of arms, scroll The three chevronells are taken from the ancient Coat of Clare, Earls of Gloucester. The golden fleeces are indicative of the wool industry. The horseshoes. The one on the dexter is taken from the ancient Arms of the City granted 20th October, 1538; the sinister one from the Arms of the Cripps family, and the centre one from the Arms of the Allen family. The demi lion and mural crown are taken from a Crest said to have been granted in the Commonwealth period to the City of Gloucester by Bysthe, Garter King of Arms. The Grants made by this King of Arms during the Commonwealth were cancelled on the Restoration of Charles II.
The Allen family motto, "Prorsum Semper" - "Ever forward".

5. *Badge worn by:* Other ranks... Standard Badge. Senior Officers... Cloth Badge.

6. *Badge fixing:* Loop and pin.

7. *Badge manufacturer:* Firmin & Son. & London Badge Co. Ltd.

8. *Badge design shown on uniform buttons:* Yes

   Badge design shown on appliances: Yes.

9. *Other particulars:* New badge incorporates the re-designed Gloucestershire Couty Crest also the name change. Title changed from 'Gloucestershire Fire Service'.

1. *Brigade:* **GREATER MANCHESTER COUNTY FIRE SERVICE**

2. **Date formed:** 1974

3. *Brigades amalgamated:* City of Salford Fire Department, Bolton, Oldham, Wigan, Bury, Rochdale, Stockport, Manchester County Borough Fire Brigades. Part of Cheshire and Lancashire County Fire Brigades.

4. *Badge design:* Home Office Star, gilt enamel Coat of Arms, scroll.
The shield bears 10 turrets in gold, representing the 10 districts of the County, on a red background. The shield is supported on each side by a lion rampant in gold. Each lion bears on its shoulder a badge in red, the lion on the right of the shield bearing a badge with a french horn representing music and culture and the lion on the left of the shield bearing a badge with an open book representing learning and the academic life of the country. The helm is surmounted by a demi-lion carrying a banner bearing 10 small turrets in gold on a red ground. The motto is 'Ever Vigilant'.

5. *Badge worn by:* Same badge worn by all ranks.

6. *Badge fixing:* Loop and pin.

7. *Badge manufacturer:*

8. *Badge design shown on uniform buttons:* Yes

   Badge design shown on appliances: Yes

9. *Other particulars:* 1st Issue. 1974-1976. Red ring, chrome letters...G.M.C.
2nd Issue. 1976   Present day badge.

1. *Brigade:* **STATES OF GUERNSEY FIRE BRIGADE.**

2. **Date formed:** Same badge since inception of brigade.

3. *Brigades amalgamated:* None.

4. *Badge design:* Home Office Star, blue ring, gilt enamel Coat of Arms. Three gilt lions on a red shield, which were the original arms of the Duchy of Normandy. The want of a Seal to make contracts and legal documents official and valid was required; on the 15th November 1279, Edward I not only granted a Seal, but sent one of his own to the Islands for the joint use of Guernsey and Jersey. In the course of time, the organisation of the Islands became more complex, and it was soon found that a common Seal for the two had its drawbacks. Around 1290 Guernsey and Jersey were granted their own Seals, the Seals were very similar in appearance, as can be seen when looking at today badges.

5. *Badge worn by:* Same badge worn by all ranks.

6. *Badge fixing:* Loop and pin.

7. *Badge manufacturer:* Fattorinn and Sons Ltd.

8. *Badge design shown on uniform buttons:* Yes

   Badge design shown on appliances: Yes.

9. *Other particulars:*

1. *Brigade:* **HAMPSHIRE FIRE BRIGADE.**

2. **Date formed:** 1974.

3. *Brigades amalgamated:* Hampshire fire service, City of Southampton and Portsmouth City fire brigades.

4. *Badge design:* Home Office star, chrome enamel shield and scroll. The present day badge is made up of the three crests of the former brigades.. Top, the red rose of Hampshire, bottom right on a blue background, a chrome moon and star. Bottom left the roses of Southampton.

5. *Badge worn by:* Same badge worn by all ranks.

6. *Badge fixing:* Loops and pin.

7. *Badge manufacturer:* Gaunts Ltd.

8. *Badge design shown on uniform buttons:* Yes

   Badge design shown on appliances: No

9. *Other particulars:*

1. *Brigade:* **HEREFORD AND WORCESTER FIRE BRIGADE**

2. **Date formed:** 1974.

3. *Brigades amalgamated:* Worcester City and County Fire Brigade, County of Hereford Fire Brigade.

4. *Badge design:* Home Office Star, red ring, chrome Coat of Arms. Shield -The three wavy lines represents the two rivers, the Severn and the Wye; the pears derive from the old Worcestershire Coat of Arms and the bull's head from the old Hertfordshire Coat of Arms. Crest - Statant upon a Mural crown a bi corporate Lion holding a pear. Supporters: On a compartment a ploughed field and a grassy mount proper, to the dexter a Talbot gorged with a collar charged with apples proper and to the sinister a Lion guardant gorged with a Wreath of Hops fructed proper.

5. *Badge worn by:* ADO and above..Embroided badge. Other ranks..standard metal badge.

6. *Badge fixing:* Loop and pin.

7. *Badge manufacturer:* Firmin and Sons Ltd.

8. *Badge design shown on uniform buttons:* Yes

   Badge design shown on appliances: Yes.

9. *Other particulars:*

1. *Brigade:* **HERTFORDSHIRE FIRE BRIGADE.**

2. **Date formed:** 1974. (Present badge issued 1975)

3. *Brigades amalgamated:* Potters Bar fire station absorbed from Middlesex.

4. *Badge design:* Home Office star. red disc, gilt deer.The Hart (adult male deer is the Hertfordshire County Council emblem. This emblem was adopted as being symbolic of this County.

5. *Badge worn by:* Same badge worn by all ranks.

6. *Badge fixing:* Loop and pin.

7. *Badge manufacturer:* Toye, Kenning Spencer.

8. *Badge design shown on uniform buttons:* No

   Badge design shown on appliances: No

9. *Other particulars:*

1. *Brigade:* **HUMBERSIDE FIRE BRIGADE.**

2. **Date formed:** 1974.

3. *Brigades amalgamated:* Kingston upon Hull, Grimsby, and part of West Riding, East Riding and Lincolnshire fire brigades.

4. *Badge design:* Home Office star. gilt and enamel shield and scroll. Crest is made up from designs of 5 previous counties that have formed Humberside. White roses of East and West Riding, Crown of Kingston upon Hull, Fleur-de-lis of Lincolnshire, Water depicting the river Humber.

5. *Badge worn by:* Same badge worn by all ranks.

6. *Badge fixing:* Loop and pin.

7. *Badge manufacturer:* Marples and Beasley Ltd.

8. *Badge design shown on uniform buttons:* Yes

   Badge design shown on appliances: Yes

9. *Other particulars:* The present cap badge design is the winner of a county badge design competition.

1. *Brigade:* **STATES OF JERSEY FIRE BRIGADE.**

2. **Date formed:** One badge design since 1950.

3. *Brigades amalgamated:* None.

4. *Badge design:* Home office star, blue ring, gilt enamel Coat of Arms. On a gilt background, a red shield bearing three Royal Leopards one above the other. The Bailiwick of Jersey has been closely linked with the English crown since the Norman Conquest of 1066. As a result of the increasing devolution of power from the Court of England, the island has had the authority to use a seal with the Royal Leopards from the regal coat of arms since 1279. The use of this seal has continued for nearly 700 years. It has become the accepted symbol of the Island.

5. *Badge worn by:* Same badge worn by all ranks.

6. *Badge fixing:* Loop and pin.

7. *Badge manufacturer:* Fattorini and sons.

8. *Badge design shown on uniform buttons:* Yes

   Badge design shown on appliances: Yes

9. *Other particulars:*

1. *Brigade:* **KENT FIRE BRIGADE.**

2. **Date formed:** 1974 (Same badge design since 1947)

3. *Brigades amalgamated:* None.

4. *Badge design:* Home office star. chrome enamel shield and scroll. The white horse rampant on a red field has for many years been the badge of Kent and tradition ascribes it to Horsa, a leader of the first Saxon settlement in England, in the Isle of Thanet.
   The motto 'INVICTA' meaning "unconquered" or "untamed", is honoured by long usage, and possibly owes its orgin to the defence put up by the community of Kent against William the Conqueror. The motto is borne upon a ribbon approximately as nearly as possible to the time-honoured Kentish Grey, a colour of significance in the days of the weaving industry in Kent.

5. *Badge worn by:* Same badge worn by all ranks.

6. *Badge fixing:* Loop and pin also single arm.

7. *Badge manufacturer:* Smith and Wright Ltd.

8. *Badge design shown on uniform buttons:* Yes

   Badge design shown on appliances: Yes.

9. *Other particulars:* The ribbon has been issued in white as well as grey.

1. *Brigade:* **LANCASHIRE COUNTY FIRE BRIGADE**

2. **Date formed:** 1974.

3. *Brigades amalgamated:* Preston, Blackburn, Burnley and Blackpool fire brigades.

4. *Badge design:* Home office star, blue ring, chrome coat of arms. A shield on which are three triangles, two from the top and one from the base, on each pile (triangle) is a rose, barbed and seeded; and for the crest, on a wreath a lion, walking with the head facing, charged on the body with a mascle (diamond shaped) and resting the right fore-paw on a shield of the arms. Supporters are on each side, a lion with a collar and hanging from it is a shield of the arms.

5. *Badge worn by:* Same badge worn by all ranks.

6. *Badge fixing:* Loop and pin.

7. *Badge manufacturer:* Gaunt and sons.

8. *Badge design shown on uniform buttons:* Yes

   Badge design shown on appliances: Yes.

9. *Other particulars:* The Lancashire County fire brigade wanted a badge simular to the police but with their crest. When the badges arrived from the manufacturer the ring was blue not red.

1. *Brigade:* **LINCOLNSHIRE FIRE BRIGADE.**

2. **Date formed:** 1974.

3. *Brigades amalgamated:* Kesteven County, Lindsey County, Lincoln City and Holland County fire brigades.

4. *Badge design:* Home Office star, red ring, chrome enamel shield. The shield which is green symbolises the green fields of Lincolnshire and carries away the diagonal band in silver (White) and blue indicative of the coastline and inland waterways network of the County, with a matching band in traditional armine symbolising Ermine Street, the Roman road which served the length of the County, in each quarter a gold fleur-de-lis taken from the arms of the city of Lincoln.

5. *Badge worn by:* D.O. and above.... badge mounted upon a circle of Laurels.

   Other ranks. ....Standard metal badge.

6. *Badge fixing:* Loop and pin.

7. *Badge manufacturer:* Firmin and Sons.

8. *Badge design shown on uniform buttons:* Yes

   Badge design shown on appliances: Yes.

9. *Other particulars:* The Lincolnshire badge has two size shields. 1st issue.. Small red ring, shield does not touch ring. 1974 to about 1980/81. 2nd issue.. Large red ring, shield touches the ring.

1. *Brigade:* **LEICESTERSHIRE FIRE BRIGADE.**

2. **Date formed:** 1974.

3. *Brigades amalgamated:* Leicester City fire brigade, and Leicestershire and Rutland fire service.

4. *Badge design:* Home Office star, red ring, chrome enamel shield. The arms were granted to the former Leicestershire County Council in 1930. The first and second quarters depict the arms of the Beaumont family, Earls of Leicester (1103-1204) and the De Montfords, Earls of Leicester (1206-1254) respectively. The third quarter represents John of Gaunt's badge granted to the County by Henry V. the Earldom of Leicester having been merged with the royal titles on the accession of Henry IV. The fourth quarter shows the badge of the Hastings family.

5. *Badge worn by:* Same badge worn by all ranks.

6. *Badge fixing:* Loop and pin.

7. *Badge manufacturer:* Gaunts and Son.

8. *Badge design shown on uniform buttons:* Yes

   Badge design shown on appliances: Yes.

9. *Other particulars:* Variation in the colour red .... dark and light red.

1. *Brigade:* **LONDON FIRE BRIGADE.**

2. **Date formed:** 1st April 1965.

3. *Brigades amalgamated:* East Ham, West Ham, Croydon, LCC London, Middlesex, fire brigades. Also parts of Essex, Kent, Surrey, and Hertfordshire fire brigades.

4. *Badge design:* Home Office star, gilt and enamel shield with a scroll.
Variations.. 1. First issue.. Chrome and enamel shield and scroll.
2. Second issue.. Gilt and enamel shield and scroll but with chrome design crown.
3. 3rd issue.... extended single arm. The lower part of the shield consists of six waved horizontal bars, this is the heraldic symbol for water and indicates London's position on the Thames. The gold crown symbolising the ancient Saxon associations of London.

5. *Badge worn by:* 1. DACO and above... Cloth badge.

   2. SDO and below... Standard metal badge.

6. *Badge fixing:* Single arm.

7. *Badge manufacturer:* Marples and Beasley.

8. *Badge design shown on uniform buttons:* Yes

   Badge design shown on appliances: Yes.

9. *Other particulars:*

41

1. *Brigade:* **ISLE OF MAN FIRE SERVICE.**

2. **Date formed:** 1965.

3. *Brigades amalgamated:* Prior to 1960 the local authorities in the island each had their own fire brigade, in 1960 six authorities merged to form the Isle of Man fire service, and in 1965 Douglas Borough also merged to form the service as now.

4. *Badge design:* Home office star, red ring, three chrome enamel legs. Three chrome legs on a red enamel background, although the motto is not shown on the badge, the three legs mean - which ever way I'm thrown I stand.

5. *Badge worn by:* Same badge worn by all ranks.

6. *Badge fixing:* Loop and pin.

7. *Badge manufacturer:* Rex Fire Protection of Leeds.

8. *Badge design shown on uniform buttons:* Yes

   Badge design shown on uniform appliance: Yes

9. *Other particulars:* Prior to the present badge being introduced there was one simular to the N.F.S. badge, but with the three legs in the centre.

1. *Brigade:* **MERSEYSIDE COUNTY FIRE BRIGADE.**

2. **Date formed:** 1974.

3. *Brigades amalgamated:* Birkenhead FB. Bootle FB. St. Helens FB. Southport FB. Wallasey CB.FB. Part Lancashire & Cheshire.

4. *Badge design:* Home Office Star. Thin red ring with buckle at bottom of ring. Ring surrounded by chrome laurel wreaths. Chrome and enamel shield on a chrome background.
   Blue enamel shield with three wavy lines from dexter chief to sinister base which represents the River Mersey. In the sinister chief and dexter base are three crowns each which depiect the six old county boroughs. Although Lancashire also made up part of this country, it was decided to only have six crowns for an even balance.

5. *Badge worn by:* Firemen.. Standard Badge.

   Badge worn by: Officers. Cloth Badge.

6. *Badge fixing:* Loop and pin.

7. *Badge manufacturer:*

8. *Badge design shown on uniform buttons:* Yes

   Badge design shown on appliances: Yes

9. *Other particulars:*

1. *Brigade:* **WEST MIDLANDS FIRE BRIGADE.**

2. **Date formed:** 1974.

3. *Brigades amalgamated:* Birmingham F&A Service. Coventry City FB. Wolverhampton F&A Service. Walsall FB. Dudley FB. Smethwick & W. Bromwich FB. Warley FB. Solihull FB. Part..Warwickshire & Worcestershire

4. *Badge design:* Home Office Star. Gilt enamel coat of arms, scroll. The gold and black of the shield represent industry. The fretwork across the centre forms the letters WM, while the bars represent strength. The supporters, two phoenix, are rising from flames symbolising rebirth and each bird has a chain around its neck which represents the chain-making industry of the West Midlands. A unique feature is the use of basket-like crowns from which the flames issue. Another unique feature is the griffin (which appears in the Coat of Arms of the Lord-Lieutenant) holding an arrow downwards. The arrow, symbolising movement, refers to the County Council being the transportation authority for its area.

5. *Badge worn by:* Same badge worn by all ranks.

6. *Badge fixing:* Loop and pin.

7. *Badge manufacturer:* Toye Kenning & Spencer.

8. *Badge design shown on uniform buttons:* Yes old design

   Badge design shown on appliances: Yes

9. *Other particulars:* 1. 1st issue worn from 1974-1981
   2. 2nd issue worn from April 1981
   1st issue was a temporary bade depicting W. Midlands County until armorial type design approved.

44

1. **Brigade:** **NORFOLK FIRE SERVICE.**

2. **Date formed:** 1974.

3. **Brigades amalgamated:** Great Yarmouth fire brigade, City of Norwich fire brigade, Norfolk fire service

4. **Badge design:** Home office star, enamel coat of arms and scroll. The arms were those of a Norman Lord, Ralph de Gauder of Waeer, who was the first to bear the titular designation of Earl of Norfolk. The chief is by way of Royal Augmentation in commemoration of His Majesty's long residence in the County as King and Prince of Wales, the lion passant guardant being taken from the Royal arms and flanked by the Prince of Wales plumes princely crowned. Dexter support - part of Great Yarmouth Coat of Arms, known as the Lion-Herring, sinister support - part of Norwich City Coat of Arms, known as Lion of Norwich. Motto 'Aestimemur Agendo' - 'Let us be Judged by our Actions'.

5. **Badge worn by:** Same badge worn by all ranks.

6. **Badge fixing:** Loop and pin.

7. **Badge manufacturer:** London badge Co. Ltd.

8. **Badge design shown on uniform buttons:** No. Crossed axes.

   Badge design shown on appliances: Yes

9. **Other particulars:** 1st Issue. Red ring with chrome shield on chrome background.
   2nd Issue. Present badge issued in 1983.

1. **Brigade:** **NORTHAMPTONSHIRE FIRE BRIGADE.**

2. **Date formed:** 1974.

3. **Brigades amalgamated:** Northampton County Borough fire brigade, Northamptonshire fire brigade.

4. **Badge design:** Home office star, chrome enamel shield and scroll. On a chrome back-ground a red Tudor rose, above a red band containing in chrome, the roses of York and Lancaster separated by a Fetterlock, all enclosed within the shield.
   The families of York and Lancaster were united by the marriage of the Earl of Richmond, the male heir of the house of Lancaster, who after his decisive victory at Bosworth, became King Henry VII, to Elizabeth, the daughter and heiress of King Edward IV by his wife, Elizabeth Woodville, and the badge adopted by King Henry VII comprising a White Rose superimposed on a Red Rose commonly called the Tudor Rose, thus became the emblem of unity and concord. The Fetterlock was a device borne by King Edward IV.

5. **Badge worn by:** Same badge worn by all ranks.

6. **Badge fixing:** Loop and pin.

7. **Badge manufacturer:** London badge co. Ltd.

8. **Badge design shown on uniform buttons:** No

   Badge design shown on appliances: No

9. **Other particulars:**

1. *Brigade:* **NORTHUMBERLAND FIRE & RESCUE SERVICE**

2. **Date formed:** Same brigade since 1947.

3. *Brigades amalgamated:* None.

4. *Badge design:* Home office star, gilt enamel coat of arms, scroll. Formerly th County Council had used the arms attributed by the medieval heralds to the ancient Kingdom of Bernicia, the Northern part of Northumbria, which was the paly of eight pieces gilt and red. It is thought that these arms were suggested by the Venerable Bede's reference to the "banner made of gold and purple" which was hung over the tomb of St. Oswald who was the first Christian King of Northumbria.

   At the time the arms were offically granted it was not possible to assign to the County Council the arms atttributed to Bernicia without change and as a result the shield was divided horizontally by an embattled line, with the paly being counter-charged in the lower part of the shield. The embattlement is thought to represent the Roman Wall and Northumberland's position as a Broder county.

   The crest refers to the old castle badge of the County Sheriffs, and the lion is that of the Percy family, Earls and later Dukes of Northumberland, Lord's Waren of the East and middle Marches. And the supporting lions are from the arms attributed to the Saint King Oswald.

5. *Badge worn by:* Senior officers... Silver & coloured embroided badge.

   Other ranks.... Standard cap badge (metal).

6. *Badge fixing:* Loop and pin.

7. *Badge manufacturer:* London badge Co. Ltd.

8. *Badge design shown on uniform buttons:* No. Council Coat of Arms.

   Badge design shown on appliances: Yes.

9. *Other particulars:* Until 1983 the brigade was known as Northumberland County Fire Brigade, in 1983 the badge was redesigned to incorporate the new title.

1. *Brigade:* **NOTTINGHAMSHIRE COUNTY FIRE BRIGADE.**

2. **Date formed:** 1974.

3. *Brigades amalgamated:* Nottingham City Fire Brigade.

4. *Badge design:* Home Office Star. Gilt enamel leaf and flames. On a red flame background a green leaf with three acorns in gilt, all above a scroll. The flames represent fire, Oak leaves and acorns represent Sherwood forest, and the blue wavy lines either side of the scroll, represent the river Trent.

5. *Badge worn by:* Same badge worn by all ranks.

6. *Badge fixing:* Loop and pin.

7. *Badge manufacturer:* Toye Kenning & Spencer.

8. *Badge design shown on uniform buttons:* Yes

   Badge design shown on appliances: Yes.

9. *Other particulars:* In 1979 the title changed from Service to Brigade on the chief officer's recommendation. He also asked members of the brigade to design a new badge. Issued in 1979.
   The first issue from 74/79 was a chrome letter 'n' on a chrome background.

1. *Brigade:* **OXFORDSHIRE FIRE SERVICE.**

2. **Date formed:** 1974.

3. *Brigades amalgamated:* Oxfordshire County fire service, The City of Oxford fire brigade, and part of Berkshire and Reading fire brigade.

4. *Badge design:* Home office star, gilt enamel coat of Arms and scroll. On the shield the silver wavy bands represent the Thames and its main tributaries, the gold wheatsheaf, and gold oak tree with acorns represent the agriculture and woods of the County. The red crown in the form of an embattled wall is an appropriate heraldic emblem for county councils. The mound, in its natural green colour, represents the Mound of Oxford Castle, the inclusion of the Castle Mound is intended to symbolise the very close connection between the Castle and the County. The Oxford Down Ram symbolises the connnection of the County with the wool trade for many hundreds of years. The ram wears a collar with a wavy band which represents the Oxfordshire rivers, as on the shield. The Ox is an allusion to Oxford's noted Ox crossing a ford. The horse has been adapted from the former Berkshire County Council's coat of arms as most of the area transferred from Berkshire is within the vale of White Horse. Like the ram in the crest, both beasts wear a wavy band collar which represents the Oxfordshire rivers. The supporters rest on a grassy mound which is broken by a central furrow and edged with earth, both as a further allusion to the importance of agriculture in Oxfordshire and to distinguish it from similar mounds in other armorial bearings.

5. *Badge worn by:* Same badge worn by all ranks.

6. *Badge fixing:* Loop and pin.

7. *Badge manufacturer:* London badge Co. Ltd.

8. *Badge design shown on uniform buttons:* Yes

   Badge design shown on appliances: Yes

9. *Other particulars:*

1. *Brigade:* **ISLES OF SCILLY FIRE BRIGADE.**

2. **Date formed:** 1947.

3. *Brigades amalgamated:* None.

4. *Badge design:* Home office star, blue ring, die pressed, enamel. The badge is a standard Brititsh fire service Association badge. The centre of the badge contains a Union Jack flying from a mast, within a laurel wreath. The blue ring contains the B.F.S.A. name and not the Brigade name.

5. *Badge worn by:* Same badge worn by all ranks.

6. *Badge fixing:* Loop and pin.

7. *Badge manufacturer:*

8. *Badge design shown on uniform buttons:* Yes with crossed axes.

Badge design shown on appliances: No.

9. *Other particulars:* 1st Issue. All chrome badge.
2nd Issue. chrome and enamel badge.

1. *Brigade:* **SHROPSHIRE FIRE SERVICE.**

2. **Date formed:** Same badge design since 1956.

3. *Brigades amalgamated:* None.

4. *Badge design:* Home office star, gilt enamel shield and scroll. A blue shield, upon it a large gilt 'W', on the arms of the W are Ermine (a fur having black spots). In the exposed sections of the shield are three leopards. The shield stands upon a scroll in red.
The leopards' faces were derived from the arms born by the corporation of Shewsbury since at least the early 15th century. Locally they are known as "the loggerheads". This orginates presumably in the practice of carving some such mofit on the head of the log used as a battering ram, their real origin is unknown. The motto - Florest Salopia - means 'May Shropshire Flourish'.

5. *Badge worn by:* Same badge worn by all ranks.

6. *Badge fixing:* Loop and pin.

7. *Badge manufacturer:* Firmin and son.

8. *Badge design shown on uniform buttons:* No old design shown.

Badge design shown on appliances: No old design shown.

9. *Other particulars:* In 1978 the brigade changed its title from 'Fire Brigade' to 'Fire Service' the new badge was issued in 1980.

1. *Brigade:* **SOMERSET FIRE BRIGADE.**

2. **Date formed:** 1974.

3. *Brigades amalgamated:* None.

4. *Badge design:* Home office star, red ring, gilt enamel shield. The arms were brought into active use on 26th November 1912. On a gilt shield a red dragon rampant, holding in its claws a blue mace erect.

5. *Badge worn by:* Same badge worn by all ranks.

6. *Badge fixing:* Loop and pin.

7. *Badge manufacturer:* Taye, Nenning & Spencer (Bedworth) Ltd.

8. *Badge design shown on uniform buttons:* Yes

   Badge design shown on appliances: Yes.

9. *Other particulars:*

1. *Brigade:* **STAFFORDSHIRE FIRE BRIGADE.**

2. **Date formed:** 1974. (Same badge design since 1947).

3. *Brigades amalgamated:* Staffordshire, City of Stoke-on-Trent, and Burton-on-Trent fire brigades.

4. *Badge design:* Home office star, red ring, Chrome shield. The shield is divided into two, On a chevron is a Stafford Knot of the first. On a chief of the second, a Lion passant and guardant of the field. The arms are composed from :- The Seal brought into being on the formation of the Staffordshire County Council in 1889 and since used by them. The field and the Chevron are the ancient arms of the family of Stafford.The Stafford Knot has, by continued use, became associated with the County and therefore occupies the honour point of the shield and makes a distinction from the Stafford family arms. The Stafford Knot has been traced back as far as 1443 on the seal of Joan, Lady of Wake.
   A Lion passant guardant, is taken from the arms recorded in the college of arms for the County Town of Stafford.

5. *Badge worn by:* Same badge worn by all ranks.

6. *Badge fixing:* Loop and pin.

7. *Badge manufacturer:* Firmin and Sons.

8. *Badge design shown on uniform buttons:* Yes

   Badge design shown on appliances: Yes.

9. *Other particulars:*

1. *Brigade:* **SUFFOLK COUNTY FIRE BRIGADE.**

2. **Date formed:** 1974.

3. *Brigades amalgamated:* Suffolk and Ipswich fire service.

4. *Badge design:* Home Office star, 3 gilt castles.The castles represents the 'Suffolk' castles.

5. *Badge worn by:* Same badge worn by all ranks.

6. *Badge fixing:* Loops and pin. Note.. badges without loops and pin are used on fire helmets.

7. *Badge manufacturer:* London badge Co. Ltd.

8. *Badge design shown on uniform buttons:* Yes
Badge design shown on appliances: Yes.

9. *Other particulars:*

1. *Brigade:* **SURREY COUNTY FIRE BRIGADE.**

2. **Date formed:** 1974.

3. *Brigades amalgamated:* Surrey fire brigade also part of Middlesex fire brigade.

4. *Badge design:* Home office star, red ring, enamel shield. Shield divided into two vertically, blue, from the arms of the Warnnes of ancient Earls of Surrey. Black, from the arms of Guildford and Godalming. Two gold crossed keys of St.Peter represent ancient power of the abbey of St. Peter in Chertsey, which owned manors extensively in the County. Keys are also in arms of Diocese of Winchester, within which much of Surrey lay and now appear in the arms of Modern Diocese of Guildford. The sprig of oak symbolising rural Surrey, was the badge of the Fitz Alans, Earls of Arundel and Surrey. The woolpack symbolising the importance of the wool trade in the County, represents the County's ancient wealth.

5. *Badge worn by:* Same badge worn by all ranks except Chief Officer, who wears a embroided badge.

6. *Badge fixing:* Loop and pin.

7. *Badge manufacturer:* London badge Co. Ltd.

8. *Badge design shown on uniform buttons:* No. S.F.B.

Badge design shown on appliances: Yes.

9. *Other particulars:* 1st Issue. Same design but without enamel. 2nd Issue.. With enamel, issued in 1975/6.

1. *Brigade:* **EAST SUSSEX FIRE BRIGADE.**

2. **Date formed:** 1974.

3. *Brigades amalgamated:* Eastbourne, Hastings, Brighton Borough fire brigades.

4. *Badge design:* Home Office star, gilt enamel shield and scroll. All on a red background, is a gilt Sussex crown and six Martlets, the Martlets have been long associated with Sussex. A horizontal wavy white line separates the crown and Martlets. The band represents the English Channel.

5. *Badge worn by:* Same badge worn by all ranks.

6. *Badge fixing:* Loops and pin.

7. *Badge manufacturer:*

8. *Badge design shown on uniform buttons:* Yes

   Badge design shown on appliances: Yes

9. *Other particulars:*

1. *Brigade:* **WEST SUSSEX FIRE BRIGADE.**

2. **Date formed:** 1974.

3. *Brigades amalgamated:* Part of East Sussex and Surrey fire brigade.

4. *Badge design:* Home Office star, red ring, crown and gilt enamel shield. The crown is taken from the East Sussex arms and the acorns from the arms of Surrey, representing the parts of those counties which have been added to West Sussex. The upper parts of blue shield has five indentations representing the five districts added to the county. The six birds are Martlets which have long been associated with Sussex. The colours are from the old West Sussex Coat of Arms.

5. *Badge worn by:* Same badge worn by all ranks.

6. *Badge fixing:* Loops and pin.

7. *Badge manufacturer:* Gaunt & Sons

8. *Badge design shown on uniform buttons:* Yes

   Badge design shown on appliances: Yes

9. *Other particulars:*

1. *Brigade:* **TYNE AND WEAR METROPOLITAN FIRE BRIGAD**

2. **Date formed:** 1974.

3. *Brigades amalgamated:* Newcastle & Gateshead fire service, Tynemouth, Sunderland, South Shield fire brigades, and parts of Durham county and Northumberland County fire brigades.

4. *Badge design:* Home Office star shape, but in a different design and in gilt, re ring, chrome enamel emblem, W on T.
The badge was designed by a member of Newcastle & Gateshead fire service... Ross Hickling.
The badge consists of a blue background with two horizontal chrome wavy lines which represent the two main rivers in the area, the centre part is the Turrett of one of the castles & the rest is the impeller of a pump.
Previous to the W on T, was the design T on W.

5. *Badge worn by:* 1. DOII & above.. Gold laurel either side of normal badge with a knot at bottom.
2. DOIII & below... standard badge.

6. *Badge fixing:* Loops and pin.

7. *Badge manufacturer:* Gaunt & Sons.

8. *Badge design shown on uniform buttons:* Yes

   Badge design shown on appliances: Yes.

9. *Other particulars:*

1. *Brigade:* **WARWICKSHIRE FIRE AND RESCUE SERVICE**

2. **Date formed:** Same badge design from 1948-1984.

3. *Brigades amalgamated:* None.

4. *Badge design:* Home Office star, oval with gilt and enamel coat of arms. The badge depicts a bear and ragged staff, and is surmounted by a castellated portcullis. These arms are taken from the Earl of Warwicks Arms.

5. *Badge worn by:* Same badge worn by all ranks.

6. *Badge fixing:* Loop and pins.

7. *Badge manufacturer:* B.H. Collins and Company Ltd.

8. *Badge design shown on uniform buttons:* Yes

   Badge design shown on appliances: Yes

9. *Other particulars:* 1st Issue. 1948/84 Badge issued in chrome and enamel as well as gilt.
2nd Issue. The brigade changed its title from 'Warwick County Fire Brigade' to its present name. only the name was changed in the new badge.

1. *Brigade:* **ISLE OF WIGHT FIRE AND RESCUE SERVICE.**

2. **Date formed:** 1947. (No change in 1974)

3. *Brigades amalgamated:* None.

4. *Badge design:* Home Office star, red ring, chrome shield. Castle represents Carisbrooke castle, the three anchors represents the ports of Yarmouth, Cowes and Bembridge, lined background represents the sea surrounding the Island.

5. *Badge worn by:* Same badge worn by all ranks.

6. *Badge fixing:* Loop and pin.

7. *Badge manufacturer:* Thomas Fatorini.

8. *Badge design shown on uniform buttons:* No. Old fire brigade design.

   Badge design shown on appliances: No. Shield only.

9. *Other particulars:* On the 1st July 1985 the title was change from 'Isle of Wight County Fire Brigade' to the new title.

1. *Brigade:* **WILTSHIRE FIRE BRIGADE.**

2. **Date formed:** Same design since 1947.

3. *Brigades amalgamated:* None.

4. *Badge design:* Home Office star, chrome enamel shield and scroll. The shield has a field or background of eight bars of white and green alternately. These were probably intended to represent the chalk and downs (chalk and cheese) of the County. In the top left hand, the shield is charged with the red dragon of Wessex of which Wilton was the ancient capital.

5. *Badge worn by:* Same badge worn by all ranks.

6. *Badge fixing:* Loops and pin.

7. *Badge manufacturer:* London Badge Co. Ltd.

8. *Badge design shown on uniform buttons:* No

   Badge design shown on appliances: No

9. *Other particulars:*

1. *Brigade:* **NORTH YORKSHIRE FIRE BRIGADE**

2. **Date formed:** 1974.

3. *Brigades amalgamated:* North, East and West Riding fire brigades also York City fire brigade.

4. *Badge design:* Home office star, red ring, chrome enamel shield. On a blue background, a white shield containing a red cross with five white Yorkshire roses upon it. Two diagonal lines of blue and green are contained within the shield.
   The red cross is that of St. George (which appeared in the arms of the former North Riding County Council and is also in the York City Arms) has been charged with five white roses, (a feature common to the Arms of all three former Riding County Councils and the City of York), The blue and green wavy bendlets represent the streams and the hills of the Dales and the Wolds.

5. *Badge worn by:* Same badge worn by all ranks.

6. *Badge fixing:* Loop and pin.

7. *Badge manufacturer:* Marples and Beasley Ltd.

8. *Badge design shown on uniform buttons:* Yes

   Badge design shown on appliances: Yes

9. *Other particulars:*

1. *Brigade:* **SOUTH YORKSHIRE COUNTY FIRE BRIGADE.**

2. **Date formed:** 1974.

3. *Brigades amalgamated:* Sheffield City fire brigade, Rotherham, Barnsley, Doncaster, county borough fire brigades, part W. Riding.

4. *Badge design:* Home Office star, red ring, gilt enamel emblem. On a gilt background, a Yorkshire rose and the letters S Y in green.

5. *Badge worn by:* Same badge worn by all ranks.

6. *Badge fixing:* Loops and pin.

7. *Badge manufacturer:* London badge Co. Ltd.

8. *Badge design shown on uniform buttons:* Yes

   Badge design shown on appliances: Yes

9. *Other particulars:*

1. *Brigade:* **WEST YORKSHIRE FIRE SERVICE.**

2. **Date formed:** 1974.

3. *Brigades amalgamated:* Bradford City FB. Leeds City FB. Wakefield City FB Dewsbury FB. Halifax FB & Huddersfield FB part.. W. Riding County.

4. *Badge design:* Home Office star. A shield in blue and gilt. The two heraldic charges on the shield form the letter 'W' the initial of 'West' and the white rose is for 'Yorkshire', thus representing heraldically the name of the county. The shield is divided into five parts which stand for the five districts, as do the petals of the rose.

5. *Badge worn by:* I. Fireman.. Standard badge.
   2. Officers.. Laurel Wreath around the H.O.S.

6. *Badge fixing:* Loop and pin.

7. *Badge manufacturer:* London badge Co. Ltd.

8. *Badge design shown on uniform buttons:* Yes old design

   Badge design shown on appliances: Yes

9. *Other particulars:* 1st Issue. worn from 1974 - 1984
   2nd issue worn from 1st April 1984

1. *Brigade:* **CENTRAL REGION FIRE BRIGADE.**

2. **Date formed:** 15th May 1975.

3. *Brigades amalgamated:* Central area. Part of Perth & Kinross fire brigades, also part of South Eastern fire brigade.

4. *Badge design:* Home Office star. Chrome coat of arms. Centre piece is regional council coat of arms comprising :- unicorn common to all new local authorities, circlet above denotes a regional authority, the Goshawk represents Perthshire, the mailed gauntlet represents Clackmannanshire, and the caltraps represent Stirlingshire. (Caltraps were used at Bannockburn by Robert the Bruce to bring down the English Horsemen.

5. *Badge worn by:* ADO & Above.. badge surrounded with oak leaves.

6. *Badge fixing:* Loop and pin.

7. *Badge manufacturer:* London badge Co. Ltd.

8. *Badge design shown on uniform buttons:* Yes

   Badge design shown on appliances: Yes

9. *Other particulars:*

1. *Brigade:* **DUMFRIES AND GALLOWAY FIRE BRIGADE.**

2. **Date formed:** May 1975.

3. *Brigades amalgamated:* Part...South Western Area.

4. *Badge design:* Home office star, red ring, gilt Coat of Arms. On a shield a cross of St. Andrew, surmounted at the centre by a shield containing a lion rampant, crowned, around the edge of main shield a counter-company border. Above the shield a Coronet appropriate to a statutory Region, which contains a circlet richly chased from which are issuant four thistles leaved. The supports stand upon a field, dexter a Stag proper, and, sinister, unicorn armed and gorged with a collar from which is pendent an oval badge, fimbriated charged with a cross of St. Andrew.

5. *Badge worn by:* ADO and above.. standard badge plus laurel wreath. Other ranks.... standard metal badge.

6. *Badge fixing:* Loop and pin.

7. *Badge manufacturer:* Gaunt & Son.

8. *Badge design shown on uniform buttons:* No

   Badge design shown on appliances: Yes

9. *Other particulars:*

1. *Brigade:* **FIFE FIRE AND RESCUE SERVICE.**

2. **Date formed:** 1974.

3. *Brigades amalgamated:* None.

4. *Badge design:* Home Office star, red ring, gilt enamel, Scottish. A heraldic jet of water playing on a fire over the Scottish national emblem (thistles in a golden field)

5. *Badge worn by:* ADO and above... have the addition of a Laurel wreath surrounding badge. Other ranks.... standard metal cap badge.

6. *Badge fixing:* Loop and pin.

7. *Badge manufacturer:* London badge Co. Ltd.

8. *Badge design shown on uniform buttons:* Yes

   Badge design shown on appliances: Yes.

9. *Other particulars:* 1st Issue. Same badge design from 1947 to 1985 - Fife fire brigade.
   2nd Issue. In 1985 brigade changed title to fire and rescue, badge design the same only name changed.

1. *Brigade:* **GRAMPIAN FIRE BRIGADE.**

2. **Date formed:** 1975.

3. *Brigades amalgamated:* North Eastern fire brigade.

4. *Badge design:* Home Office Star. red ring, chrome Coat of Arms. The Armorial Bearings were granted to Grampion Regional Council by Scotland's heraldic authority, the Lord Lyon King of Arms, in 1975. They comprise a St. Andrew's Cross on a shield surmounted by a small shield bearing a cross. Above the shield is a coronet appropriate to a statutory Region. Issuing from the coronet are thistles.
Supporting the shield are, on the left, a ptarmigan (bird of grouse family), and, on the right, a unicorn, armed maned and with a collar from which hangs on an oval badge bearing a Saltire (diagonal cross).

5. *Badge worn by:* ADO and above... Cloth embroided badge.
Other ranks ...Standard metal badge.

6. *Badge fixing:* Loop and pin.

7. *Badge manufacturer:* Gaunt and Son.

8. *Badge design shown on uniform buttons:* Yes

   Badge design shown on appliances: Yes

9. *Other particulars:*

1. *Brigade:* **HIGHLAND & ISLANDS FIRE BRIGADE.**

2. **Date formed:** 1975.

3. *Brigades amalgamated:* None.

4. *Badge design:* Home Office star, red ring, gilt enamel, Scottish. A heraldic jet of water playing on a fire over the Scottish national emblem. (Thistles in a golden field).

5. *Badge worn by:* 1. Fireman.. Standard badge.
2. Officers badge.. Standard badge positioned on a silver metal laurel wreath.
3. Senior officers.. as above but woven on gold & silver thread.

6. *Badge fixing:* Loop and pin.

7. *Badge manufacturer:* London badge Co. Ltd.

8. *Badge design shown on uniform buttons:* Yes

   Badge design shown on appliances: Yes

9. *Other particulars:* 1st Issue.. 1975 ..Northern Fire Brigade
Name was not felt to clearly project the identity of the area served, hence the change in 1983. Badge design stayed the same, only the title was changed.

1. *Brigade:* **LOTHIAN AND BORDERS FIRE BRIGADE.**

2. **Date formed:** 1975.

3. *Brigades amalgamated:* Change of name from South Eastern fire brigade.

4. *Badge design:* Home Office star, red ring, gilt enamel, Scottish. A heraldic je of water playing on a fire over the Scottish national emblem, (Thistles in a golden field).

5. *Badge worn by:* ADO & above.. badge surrounded by Laurel leaves.
   2. Stn.O. & below.. standard metal badge.

6. *Badge fixing:* Loops and pin.

7. *Badge manufacturer:* Firmin and Sons.

8. *Badge design shown on uniform buttons:* Yes

   Badge design shown on appliances: Yes.

9. *Other particulars:*

1. *Brigade:* **STRATHCLYDE FIRE BRIGADE.**

2. **Date formed:** 16th May 1975

3. *Brigades amalgamated:* Glasgow, Lanarkshire, Western area fire brigades, part of Central Area and South Western area fire brigades.

4. *Badge design:* Home Office star, red ring, gilt enamel, Scottish. A heraldic jet of water playing on a fire over the Scottish national emblem, (thistles in a golden field).

5. *Badge worn by:* Ass't. firemaster to firemaster.. embroided badge.
   ADO - SDO .... standard cap badge surrounded by Laurel Wreath.
   Other ranks... standard cap badge.

6. *Badge fixing:* Loop and pin.

7. *Badge manufacturer:* J.R. Gaunt and Son.

8. *Badge design shown on uniform buttons:* Yes, inner circle only.

   Badge design shown on appliances: Yes.

9. *Other particulars:*

1. *Brigade:* **TAYSIDE FIRE BRIGADE.**

2. **Date formed:** May 1975.

3. *Brigades amalgamated:* Angus area fire brigade and Perth & Kinross fire brigades.

4. *Badge design:* Home Office Star. red ring, gilt enamel, Scottish. A heraldic jet of water playing on a fire over the Scottish national emblem, (thistles in a golden field).

5. *Badge worn by:* ADO and above ...standard badge surrounded by laurel leaves.
Other ranks ...standard cap badge.

6. *Badge fixing:* Loop and pin.

7. *Badge manufacturer:* London badge Co. Ltd.

8. *Badge design shown on uniform buttons:* Yes

   Badge design shown on appliances: Yes

9. *Other particulars:*

1. *Brigade:* **NORTHERN IRELAND FIRE BRIGADE.**

2. **Date formed:** October 1973.

3. *Brigades amalgamated:* Belfast fire brigade and Northern Ireland Fire authority.

4. *Badge design:* Home Office star, red ring, star plus red hand. Inner ring in green enamel (Ireland) with chrome six pointed star of Northern Ireland with insert of red hand of Ulster. Badge thus incorporated the two former brigades.

5. *Badge worn by:* D.O. and above... cloth embroided badge.
Other ranks ...standard metal badge.

6. *Badge fixing:* Loop and pin.

7. *Badge manufacturer:* London badge Co. Ltd.

8. *Badge design shown on uniform buttons:* Yes

   Badge design shown on appliances: No. Fire brigade has its own Coat of Arms.

9. *Other particulars:* In 1973 the badge was a one piece badge and about 1980 the badge changed into a two piece badge. In 1984 on the Chief Officers instructions the name changed from 'Fire Authority for Northern Ireland' to its present name.
The badge design stayed the same but the name around the red ring was changed.

1. *Brigade:* **COUNTY OF CLWYD FIRE SERVICE.**

2. **Date formed:** 1974.

3. *Brigades amalgamated:* County of Flintshire fire service, part Denbighshire and Montgomeryshire joint fire service.

4. *Badge design:* Home office star, chrome enamel shield. The shield combines elements from the arms of the former Flintshire and Denbighshire County Councils. The wave represents the Vale of Clwyd and the Clwydian hills lying between the two counties. The cross and choughs from the Flintshire shield come from the traditional arms of Edwin of Tegeingl, founder of the twelfth Noble Tribe of North Wales. The black lion of the Princes of Powys Fadog comes from the Denbighshire shield.

5. *Badge worn by:* Same badge worn by all ranks.

6. *Badge fixing:* Loop and pin.

7. *Badge manufacturer:* Gaunt and son.

8. *Badge design shown on uniform buttons:* Yes

   Badge design shown on appliances: Yes

9. *Other particulars:*

1. *Brigade:* **DYFED COUNTY FIRE BRIGADE.**

2. **Date formed:** 1974.

3. *Brigades amalgamated:* Carmarthenshire & Cardiganshire joint fire brigade, and Pembrokeshire fire brigade.

4. *Badge design:* Home office Star, red ring, Chrome enamel shield. The shield is divided into three parts. In the first is a golden lion rampant regardant on a black ground for Gwaethfoed. Prince of Ceredigion, from the arms of the former Cardiganshire County Council. In the second is a golden lion rampant on a red ground within a golden border for Rhys ap Tewdwr, Prince of Deheubarth, from the arms of the former Carmarthenshire County Council. The third is a golden lion rampant between golden roses on a blue ground, representing Gwynfardd, Prince of Dyfed, whose seat was Pembrokeshire. The whole signifies the earliest form of local government in the area, represented today by Dyfed County Council, a tradition of over a thousand years.

5. *Badge worn by:* Same badge worn by all ranks.

6. *Badge fixing:* Loop and pin.

7. *Badge manufacturer:* London badge Co. Ltd.

8. *Badge design shown on uniform buttons:* Yes

   Badge design shown on appliances: Yes

9. *Other particulars:*

1. *Brigade:* **MID GLAMORGAN FIRE SERVICE.**

2. **Date formed:** 1974.

3. *Brigades amalgamated:* Part of Monmouthshire, Breconshire and Radnorshire, and Merthyr Tydfil fire brigades, part Glamorgan fire service.

4. *Badge design:* Home Office star, gilt enamel shield and dragon. The badge is composed of two elements, the clarion of the De Clare family (Norman Lord of the medievel marcher Lordship of Glamorgan, who held power from 1217 to 1317) encircles the single Tudor rose of Mid Glamorgan, (Tudor rose is symbolic of the creation of the shire by Henry VIII in 1536). The crest, surmounting the helmet and wreath of gold and red, is a red demi dragon, symbolic of the land of Wales. The banner which it holds triumphantly, carries three silver chevronels on a red field, the arms attributed to Jestyn ap Gwrgant, the last Welsh ruler of Morgannwg. With elevated wings and issuing from flames, the demi dragon also symbolises the revival of the area after a long period of depression, which suggestion is borne out in the motto.

5. *Badge worn by:* 1. DO I and above .. cloth badge.
   2. DOII and below... standard metal badge.

6. *Badge fixing:* Loops and pin.

7. *Badge manufacturer:* Dowler.

8. *Badge design shown on uniform buttons:* Yes

   Badge design shown on appliances: Yes

9. *Other particulars:*

1. *Brigade:* **SOUTH GLAMORGAN FIRE SERVICE**

2. **Date formed:** 1974.

3. *Brigades amalgamated:* Cardiff City fire service and Glamorgan fire service.

4. *Badge design:* Home office star, gilt enamel Coat of Arms. On the shield, the strongest mofit is a roundel bearing three chevrons in one half the red chevrons of the de Clare family, Norman Lords of Glamorgan (who made Cardiff the centre of their Lordship), and in the other half the three silver chevrons attributed to Iestyn ap Gwrgant, the last Welsh ruler of Morgannwg. The roundel is crowned, as a symbol that it represents the capital city which is contained within the new county. On the ground of the shield the ermine pile inverted refers to the rich valley guarded by castles, which are shown above on either side.
The crest consists of a mural crown, appropriate to county councils, with emerging from it a mitre, the chief symbol in the arms of the See of Llandaff,. an allusion to the cathedral church of Llandaff.
The supporters, the heraldic beasts holding the shield, are the red dragon of Wales and the red lion of the Princes of South Wales. Their wings symbolise the county's links with the air at Rhoose and St. Athan and they hold tridents to show the county's strong connection with the sea.

5. *Badge worn by:* Senior officers...Wire embroided badge.
Other ranks ...Standard metal badge.

6. *Badge fixing:* Loop and pin.

7. *Badge manufacturer:* Maples and Beasley.

8. *Badge design shown on uniform buttons:* No

   Badge design shown on appliances: No. Only Coat of Arms.

9. *Other particulars:* 1st Issue... 1974-76 Coat of Arms direct onto eight pointed star. (In brass)
2nd Issue... Coat of arms with enamel inserted.

1. *Brigade:* **WEST GLAMORGAN COUNTY FIRE BRIGADE.**

2. **Date formed:** 1974.

3. *Brigades amalgamated:* Swansea City fire brigade and part of Glamorgan County fire brigade.

4. *Badge design:* Home office star, gilt enamel coat arms, scroll. A white shield with three chevronels, being the traditional arms of the old Princes of Gwry, also on the shield - two pine cones and a liquid drop. The liquid drop refers to the coal, oil refining and attendant industries. The pine cones and liquid drop form a convenient allusion of country side with urban areas. The crest consists of a demi-Welsh dragon holding between its paws a tudor rose. This whole device rises behind four annuletes embattled on the outer edge all coloured gold. These refer to the four Districts which make up the County and the annuletes refer to the industries of each. Left supporter is an Osprey holding a fish in its beak, being forna known to the area. Around its neck is a chain of steel links in reference to the importance of the steel industry to the area. The right supporter consists of a heron with an aluminium collar about its neck representing the aluminium industry, the heron holds in its beak a fish. The fish of the two supporters refer to the maritime interest of the area. The base under the supporters - consists of water to the left being a further reference to the maritime interests and the water harbour for which the area is famous; the other part of the compartment consists of a ploughed field and is a reference to the importance of agriculture in the area.
The Helm is that appropriate to a Corporation; the mantling and Crest wreath in the national colours of Wales - Green and White.

5. *Badge worn by:* Same badge worn by all ranks.

6. *Badge fixing:* Loop and pin.

7. *Badge manufacturer:* London badge Co. Ltd.

8. *Badge design shown on uniform buttons:* No

   Badge design shown on appliances: Yes

9. *Other particulars:* From 1974 to 1978/9 the Swansea and Glamorgan badges were still worn by the men from those brigades. In 1978/9 the new design was issued, 1st issue... in Chrome, 2nd issue ....in gilt.

1. *Brigade:* **GWENT FIRE BRIGADE.**

2. **Date formed:** 1974.

3. *Brigades amalgamated:* Newport CB. FS. Monmouthshire FB.

4. *Badge design:* Home Office star, enamel coat of arms. The gold fleurs-de-lis upon blue and black are the arms of the ancient Kingdom of Gwent. The castles are the arms of the ancient Princes of Gwent and also refer to the many castles situated in the county. The motto 'Utrique Fidelis' (Faithful to Both) shows the county as faithful to both England and Wales, and the gold lion of England and the red dragon of Wales each holding its country's National Emblem illustrae this double allegiance. The Somerset Coat of Arms, shown on the castle forming the crest, refers to the connections of the Somerset family with the county.

5. *Badge worn by:* Same badge worn by all ranks.

6. *Badge fixing:* Loop and pin.

7. *Badge manufacturer:* London badge Co. Ltd.

8. *Badge design shown on uniform buttons:* Yes

   Badge design shown on appliances: Yes

9. *Other particulars:* 1st Issue. 1974 - 1982
   2nd Issue. 1982.

1. *Brigade:* **GWYNEDD FIRE SERVICE.**

2. **Date formed:** 1974. (Badge issued 1976)

3. *Brigades amalgamated:* Anglesey Fire Department, Merioneth Fire Service, County of Caervarvon fire service.

4. *Badge design:* Home office star, red ring, chrome enamel shield. the shield is upon a chrome background, the shield chief contains three squares, the two red lions passant on a yellow background come from the arms of Caernarfonshire, the golden lion rampant on a red background in the centre from the arms of Anglesey, with the goat on the blue background underneath coming from the Merioneth arms.

5. *Badge worn by:* ADO and above ... standard metal badge with chrome laurel wreath surround.
   Other ranks .... standard metal badge.

6. *Badge fixing:* Loop and pin.

7. *Badge manufacturer:* Gaunt and sons.

8. *Badge design shown on uniform buttons:* No. Helmet & crossed axes.

   Badge design shown on appliances: No. Full Coat of Arms (County crest).

9. *Other particulars:*

1. *Brigade:* **POWYS FIRE SERVICE**

2. **Date formed:** 1974

3. *Brigades amalgamated:* Breconshire and Radnorshire Joint Fire Brigade, Montgomeryshire Fire Brigade.

4. *Badge design:* Home Office Star, white disc and dragon. On a white enamel background stands a Welsh dragon in the passant position. The dragon stands upon a base of red and yellow flames.

5. *Badge worn by:* Same badge worn by all ranks.

6. *Badge fixing:* Loop and pin.

7. *Badge manufacturer:* Firmin and Son.

8. *Badge design shown on uniform buttons:* Yes

   Badge design shown onappliances: Yes

9. *Other particulars:* This badge has been issued in gilt and chrome.

1. *Brigade:* **FIRE SERVICE COLLEGE (MORETON-IN-MARSH, GLOUCESTERSHIRE)**

2. **Date formed:** 1981

3. *Brigades amalgamated:* 1951 Fire Service Training Centre
1968 Fire Service Technical College.

4. *Badge design:* Seven Pointed Star surmounted by the Royal Crown. Red ring with Fire Service College in chrome surrounding the Royal Cipher.

5. *Badge worn by:* Same badge worn by all ranks.

6. *Badge fixing:* Loop and pin.

7. *Badge manufacturer:* William Dowler Ltd.

8. *Badge design shown on uniform buttons:* No

   Badge design shown on appliances: Yes

9. *Other particulars:* In 1981 the Fire Service Staff College, Dorking, amalgamated with the Fire Service Technical College to form the Fire Service College. The Fire Service College is a Home Office establishment for the British Fire Service to provide centralised officer training on a progressive basis from the most junior rank of leading fireman through to Chief officer. Training is also provided for overseas fire brigades and for industry and commerce.
The college, which has a capacity for 470 residential students, is unique in the scale and sophistication of the training provided in technical, supervisory and managerial studies for fire service officers.

1. *Brigade:* **PETERBOROUGH VOLUNTEER FIRE BRIGADE**

2. **Date formed:** 1884 (1947 became part of the County Fire Fighting Force)

3. *Brigades amalgamated:* None

4. *Badge design:* Home Office Star, red ring, chrome enamel shield. The circle containing the wording "Peterborough Volunteer Fire Brigade" is on a red background, the crossed keys symbol is also on a red background whereas the crossed swords are on a pale blue background. The infill between the centre shield and the circular name is in black. The crossed keys represent the Bishopric or See of Peterborough and these are also used by the city in their Coat of Arms. The crossed swords represent the Dean and Chapter.

5. *Badge worn by:* Chief Officer.. Silver British Fire Service Assn. surround with Peterborough Vol. centre. Second Officer..Bronze B.F.S.A. surround with Peterborough Vol. centre. Other ranks..Standard metal badge.

6. *Badge fixing:* Loop and pin.

7. *Badge manufacturer:* London badge Co. Ltd.

8. *Badge design shown on uniform buttons:* No

   Badge design shown on appliances: No. Cambridgeshire County badge

9. *Other particulars:* This is the only Volunteer brigade in the country, members receive no payment for services, and man two appliances. The brigade has maintained its own identity since 1884.

Anglesey Fire Department.	Gwynedd FS.
Angus Area FB.	Tayside FB.
Barnsley CB. FB.	South Yorkshire County FS.
Barrow-In-Furrness CB. FB.	Cumbria FS.
Bath FB.	County of Avon FB.
Bath Fire & Ambulance Service.	" " " "
Bedfordshire FS.	
Belfast Fire Authority.	Bedfordshire FS.
Belfast FB.	Northern Island FB.
	" " "
Berkshire & Reading FB. (PT)	Royal Berkshire F & R.S.
" " " (PT)	Hampshire FB.
Birkenhead FB.	Merseyside CFB.
Birmingham Fire & Ambulance Service.	West Midlands County FS.
Blackburn FB.	Lancashire C.FB.
Blackpool FB.	" "
Bolton FB.	Greater Manchester C.FS.
Bootle FB.	Merseyside C.FB.
Bournmouth FB.	Dorset FB.
Bradford City FB.	West Yorkshire FS.
Bradford FB.	" " "
Breconshire & Radnorshire C.FB.	Powys FS.
Brighton FB.	East Sussex FB.
Bristol, City & County of,	County of Avon FB.
Buckinghamshire FB. (PT)	Royal Berkshire F & RS.
" " (PT)	Buckinghamshire FB.
Burnley FB.	Lancashire C.FB.
Burton-On-Trent FB.	Staffordshire FB.
Bury FB.	Greater Manchester C.FS.
Caernarvon, County of, FS.	Gwynedd FS.
Cambridge & Isle of Ely C.FB.	Cambridgeshire F & RS.
Cambridgeshire FB.	" "
Cardiff City FS.	South Glamorgan FS.
Carlisle FB.	Cumbria FS.
Carmarthenshire & Cardiganshire JFB.	Dyfed. C.FB.
Central Area FB.	Strathclyde FB.
Central FB.	Central FB.
Cheshire C.FB. (PT)	Cheshire FB.
" " (PT)	Greater Manchester C.FS.
Chester City F.S.	Cheshire FB.
Cornwall FB.	Cornwall C.FB.
Coventry City FB.	West Midlands FS.
Croydon FB.	London FB.
Cumberland FS.	Cumbria FS.
Cumberland & Westmorland FB.	" "
Darlington FB.	Durham C.FB.
Denbighshire & Montgomeryshire JFS.	Powys FS.
Derby CB. FB.	Derbyshire FS.
Devon C.FS.	Devon FB.
Dewsbury FB.	West Yorkshire FS.
Doncaster FB.	South Yorkshire FS.

Dorset C.FS.	Dorset FB.
Dudley Fire & Ambulance Service.	West Midlands FS.
Durham C.FB. (PT)	Durham C.FB.
" " (PT)	Tyne & Wear Metropolitan FB.
Denbighshire FS.	Clwyd FS.
Eastbourne FB.	East Sussex FB.
Eastern FA.	Northern Ireland FB.
East Ham FB.	London FB.
East Riding C.FB. (PT)	Humberside C.FB.
" " " (PT)	North Yorkshire FB.
East Sussex FB. (PT)	West Sussex FB.
" " (PT)	East Sussex FB.
Ely, Isle of, FS.	Cambridgeshire F & RS.
Essex C.FB. (PT)	London FB.
" " (PT)	Essex County F & RS.
Exeter FB.	Devon FB.
Fire Authority For Northern Ireland	Northern Ireland FB.
Fife FB.	Fife F & RS.
Flintshire C.FB.	Clwyd FS.
Glamorgan FS. (PT)	West Glamorgan C.FS.
Glasgow FS.	Strathclyde FB.
Gloucester City FS.	Gloucestershire F & RS.
Gloucestershire FB. (PT)	County of Avon FB.
Grampian FB.	Grampian FB.
Great Yarmouth FB	Norfolk FS.
Grimsby FB.	Humberside C.FB.
Guernsey, States of, FB.	Guernsey, States of, FB.
Halifax FB.	West Yorkshire FS.
Hampshire FS.	Hampshire FB.
Hartlepool FB.	Cleveland C.FB.
Hastings FB.	East Sussex FB.
Herefordshire, County of, FB.	Hereford & Worcester FB.
Hertfordshire FB. (PT)	London FB.
" " (PT)	Hertfordshire FB.
Holland C.FB.	Lincolnshire FB.
Huddersfield FB.	West Yorkshire FS.
Huntingdon County FS.	Cambridge F & RS.
Huntingdon & Petersborough FB.	" "
Jersey, States of, FB.	Jersey, States of, FB.
Kent FB. (PT)	London FB.
" (PT)	Kent FB.
Kesteven C.FB.	Lincolnshire FB.
Kingston-Upon-Hull FB.	Humberside C.FB.
Lanlarkshire FB.	Strathclyde FB.
Lancashire C.FB. (PT)	Lancashire C.FB.
" " (PT)	Greater Manchester C.FS.
" " (PT)	Cumbria FS.
Leeds City FB.	West Yorkshire FS.
Leicester City FB.	Leicestershire FB.

Leicestershire & Rutland FS.	Leicestershire FB.
Lincoln City FB.	Lincolnshire FB.
Lincolnshire FB.	Humberside C.FB.
Lindsey C.FB.	Lincolnshire F.B.
Lincolnshire FB.	" "
Liverpool, City of, FB.	Merseyside C.FB.
" " FS.	" "
London - LCC - FB.	London FB.
Luton FB.	Bedfordshire FS.
Manchester CB. FB.	Greater Manchester C.FS.
Man, Isle of, FB.	Man, Isle of, FB.
Merioneth FS.	Gwynedd FS.
Merthyr Tydfill FB.	Mid Glamorgan FS.
Middlesborough FB.	Cleveland C.FB.
Middlesex FB.	London FB.
Monmouthshire FB.	Mid Glamorgan FS.
Montgomershire FS.	Powys FS.
Newcastle & Gateshead FS.	Tyne & Wear Metropolitan FB.
Newport CB. FS.	Gwent FB.
Norfolk FS.	Norfolk FS.
Northamptonshire FB.	Northamptonshire. FB.
Northampton CB.FB.	" "
North Eastern FB.	Grampian FB.
Northern FA.	Northern Ireland FB.
Northern FB.	Highland & Islands FB.
Northern Area FB.	" "
Northern Ireland FA.	Northern Ireland FB.
North Riding FB.	North Yorkshire FB.
Northumberland C.FB. (PT)	Tyne & Wear Metropolitan FB.
" " (PT)	Northumberland F & RS.
Norwich, City of, FB.	Norfolk FS.
Nottingham City FB.	Nottinghamshire FB.
Nottinghamshire FS.	" "
Oldham FB.	Greater Manchester C.FS.
Oxfordshire C.FS. (PT)	Oxfordshire FS.
" " (PT)	Hampshire FB.
Oxford, City of, FB.	Oxfordshire FS.
Pembrokshire FB.	Dyfed C.FB.
Peterborough Volunteer FB.	Petersborough Volunteer FB.
Peterborough, Soke of, FB.	Cambridgeshire F & RS.
Perth & Kinross FB. (PT)	Tayside FB.
" " (PT)	Central Region FB.
Preston FB.	Lancashire C.FB.
Portsmouth City FB.	Hampshire FB.
Plymouth City FB.	Devon FB.
Rochdale CB. FB.	Greater Manchester C.FS.
Rotherham CB. FB.	South Yorkshire FS.
Royal Berkshire FB.	Royal Berkshire F & RS.

alford, City of, FD.	Greater Manchester C.FS.
cilly, Isle of, FB.	Scilly, Isle of, FB.
heffield FB.	South Yorkshire FS.
hropshire FB.	Shropshire FS.
methwick & West Bromwich. FS.	West Midland FS.
	" " "
olihull FB.	
omerset FB. (PT)	County of Avon FB.
" " (PT)	Somerset FB.
outhampton, City of, FB.	Hampshire FB.
outhampton FB.	" "
outh Eastern FB. (PT)	Lothian & Borders FB.
" " " (PT)	Central Region FB.
outhend-On-Sea CB.FB.	Essex County F & RS.
outhern FA.	Northern Ireland FB.
outhshields FB.	Tyne & Wear Metropolitan FB.
outhport FB.	Merseyside C.FB.
outh Western Area FB.	Dumfries & Galloway FB.
taffordshire FB.	Staffordshire FB.
tockport FB.	Greater Manchester C.FS.
toke-On-Trent, City, FB.	Staffordshire FB.
t. Helens FB.	Merseyside C.FB.
uffolk & Ipswich FS.	Suffolk FS.
underland FB.	Tyne & Wear Metropolitan FB.
urrey FB. (PT)	Surrey FB.
" " (PT)	London FB.
wansea FB.	West Glamorgan C.FS.
Teeside FB.	Cleveland C.FB.
Tynemouth FB.	Tyne & Wear Metropolitan FB.
Wakefield City FB.	West Yorkshire FS.
Walsall FB.	West Midlands FS.
Wallasey, CB of, FB.	Merseyside C.FB.
Warley FB.	West Midlands FS.
Warrington FB.	Cheshire FB.
Warwick C.FB.	Warwickshire F & RS.
West Bromich FB.	West Midlands FS.
Western Area FB.	Strathclyde FB.
Western FA.	Northern Ireland FB.
West Ham FB.	London FB.
West Hartlepool FB.	Cleveland C.FB.
Westmorland FB.	Cumbria FS.
West Riding C.FB. (PT)	South Yorkshire FS.
" " " (PT)	Humberside C.FB.
" " " (PT)	North Yorkshire FB.
" " " (PT)	Cumbria FS.
West Sussex FB.	West Sussex FB.
Wigan FB.	Greater Manchester C.FS.
Wiltshire FB.	Wiltshire C.FB.
Wight, Isle of, FB	Wight, Isle of, F & R.S.
Wolverhampton Fire & Rescue Service.	West Midlands FS.
Worcester City & County FB.	Hereford & Worcester FB.
York FB.	North Yorkshire FB.

C.FB.	County Fire Brigade.
C.FS.	County Fire Service.
CB.FB.	County Borough Fire Brigade.
FA.	Fire Authority.
FB.	Fire Brigade.
F & RS.	Fire and Rescue Service.
JFB.	Joint Fire Brigade.
JFS.	Joint Fire Service.
PT.	Part.

RECENT CHANGES

RETITLED BRIGADES

From —	To —
* Royal Berkshire FB.	Royal Berkshire Fire & Rescue Service.
* Essex County FB.	Essex County Fire & Rescue Service.
Fire Authority for Northern Ireland	Northern Ireland Fire Brigade.
Gloucestershire FS.	Gloucestershire Fire & Rescue Service.
Northern FB.	Highland & Islands FB.
Northumberland FB.	Northumberland Fire & Rescue Service.
Shropshire FB.	Shropshire FS.
* Warwick County FB.	Warwickshire Fire & Rescue Service.
* Wight, Isle of, FB.	Wight, Isle of, Fire & Rescue Service.
Fife FB.	Fife Fire & Rescue Service.
Nottinghamshire FS.	Nottinghamshire FB.

(*Denotes that a new badge design is in the process.)

Redesigned Badges.

Derbyshire FS.
Greater Manchester C.FS.
Gwent FB.
Merseyside FB.
Norfolk FS.
Nottinghamshire FB.
West Glamorgan FS.
West Midlands C.FS.
West Yorkshire FS.

Avon Fire Brigade
HOS R/R C/E Sea Stag.
Bedfordshire Fire Service
HOS R/R G/E SH
Royal Berkshire Fire & Rescue Service
HOS R/R C/E C/A
HOS R/R C   C/A
Buckinghamshire Fire Brigade
HOS white/R Swan Plastic cover
HOS white/R G/E Swan
HOS white/R C/E Swan
Cambridgeshire Fire and Rescue Service
HOS G/E SCR
Cheshire Fire Brigade
HOS R/R G/E SH
Cleveland Fire Brigade
HOS G/E SH SCR
Cornwall Fire Brigade
HOS C/E SH Black SCR
Cumbria Fire Service
HOS C/E SH SCR
HOS lge C/E SH SCR
Derbyshire Fire Service
HOS R/R C SH
HOS G/E C/A SCR
Devon Fire Brigade
HOS R/R C/E C/A
Dorset Fire Brigade
HOS R/R C SH
Durham County Fire Brigade
HOS G/E SH SCR. White Rose
Essex County Fire and Rescue Service
HOS C/E SH SCR
HOS G/E SH SCR
Gloucestershire Fire and Rescue Service
HOS R/R C SH SCR
HOS G/E C/A SCR
Greater Manchester Fire Service
LHOS R/R C Lttrs GMC
HOS G/E C/A SCR
Hampshire Fire Brigade
HOS G/E SH SCR

Hereford and Worcester Fire Brigade
HOS R/R C/A
Hertfordshire Fire Brigade
LHOS R/D G Deer
Humberside Fire Brigade
HOS G/E SH SCR
Kent Fire Brigade
HOS C/E SH SCR
HOS C/E SH GR SCR
Lancashire County Fire Brigade
HOS B/R C C/A
Leicestershire Fire Brigade
HOS LR/R C/E SH
Lincolnshire Fire Brigade
HOS small R/R C/E SH
Hos large R/R C/E SH
London Fire Brigade
HOS C/E SH SCR
HOS G/E SH SCR
Merseyside County Fire Brigade
HOS WR/R Helmet and Axes
HOS W/Thin R/R C/E SH
Norfolk Fire Service
HOS R/R C SH
HOS C/E C/A SCR
Northamptonshire Fire Brigade
HOS C/E SH SCR
Northumberland Fire and Rescue Service
HOS G/E C/A SCR (FB)
HOS G/E C/A SCR
Nottinghamshire Fire Brigade
HOS R/R C/E Lttr n
HOS G/E Leaf/Flame SCR
Oxfordshire Fire Service
G/E C/A SCR
Shropshire Fire Service
HOS G/E SH SCR
HOS G/E SH SCR (BRIGADE)
Isles of Scilly Fire Brigade
HOS B/R C/E WREATH/FLAG
Somerset Fire Brigade
R/R G/E SH

Staffordshire Fire Brigade
HOS R/R C SH
Suffolk Fire Service
HOS 3 G CASTLES
Surrey Fire Brigade
HOS R/R C SH
HOS R/R C/E SH
East Sussex Fire Brigade
HOS G/E SH SCR
HOS G/E SH WAVY LINE
West Sussex Fire Brigade
HOS R/R Crown G/E SH
Tyne and Wear Metropolitan Fire Brigade
G ST R/R SCR C/E emblem T on W
G ST R/R SCR C/E emblem W on T
Warwickshire Fire and Rescue Service
HOS OV C/E C/A (FB)
HOS OV G/E C/A (FB)
HOS OV C/E C/A
West Midlands County Fire Service
HOS Plastic Cover R/R C/E Map
HOS R/R C/E MAP (Thin)
HOS R/R C/E MAP (Thick)
HOS G/E C/A SCR
Isle of White Fire and Rescue Service
HOS R/R C/A (FB)
Wiltshire Fire Brigade
HOS C/E SH SCR
North Yorkshire Fire Brigade
HOS R/R C/E SH
South Yorkshire Fire Service
HOS R/R G/E EMBLEM
West Yorkshire Fire Service
HOS R/R C/E EMBLEM
HOS G/E SH
Isle of Man Fire Service
HOS R/R C/E 3 LEGS
States of Jersey Fire Service
HOS BL/R G/E SH
States of Guernsey Fire Brigade
HOS BL/R G/E SH

Clwyd Fire Service
HOS C/E SH
Dyfed Fire Brigade
HOS R/R C/E SH
Mid Glamorgan Fire Service
HOS G/E SH Dragon
South Glamorgan Fire Service
HOS G/E C/A
HOS G/E C/A (BRASS)
West Glamorgan Fire Service
HOS G/E C/A SCR
HOS C/E C/A SCR
Gwent Fire Brigade
HOS G/E SH SCR
HOS G/E C/A SCR
Gwynedd Fire Service
R/R C/E SH
Powys Fire Service
HOS WH DISC DRAGON
Central Region Fire Brigade
HOS C C/A
Dumfries and Galloway Fire Brigade
HOS R/R G C/A
Fife Fire Brigade
HOS G/E SCOTTISH
Grampian Fire Brigade
HOS R/R C C/A
Lothian and Borders
HOS R/R G/E SCOTTISH
Highland and Islands
(Was NORTHERN)
HOS R/R C SCOTTISH
HOS R/R C/E SCOTTISH
Strathclyde Fire Brigade
HOS R/R G/E SCOTTISH
HOS R/R C/E SCOTTISH
Tayside Fire Brigade
HOS R/R G/E SCOTTISH
Northern Ireland Fire Brigade
(Was F.A.N.I.)
HOS R/R C/E RED HAND
HOS R/R C/E RED HAND

ABBREVIATIONS.
HOS   HOME OFFICE STAR
S   SMALL
R/R   RED RING
G   GILT
E   ENAMEL
SH   SHIELD
SCR   SCROLL
C   CHROME
Lttrs   LETTERS
OV   OVAL
GR   GREY
G ST   GILT STAR
FB   FIRE BRIGADE
WH   WHITE
FANI FIRE AUTHORITY NORTHERN IRELAND